Featherstone

fantastic ideas for
promoting independence

ALISTAIR BRYCE-CLEGG

Published 2013 by Featherstone Education
Bloomsbury Publishing plc
50 Bedford Square, London, WC1B 3DP
www.bloomsbury.com

ISBN 978-1-4081-7954-3

Text © Alistair Bryce-Clegg 2013
Design © Lynda Murray
Photographs © Shutterstock

Printed and bound in China by C&C Offset Printing Co. Ltd., Shenzen, Guangdong

This book is produced using paper that is made from wood grown in
managed, sustainable forests. It is natural, renewable and recyclable.
The logging and manufacturing processes conform to the environmental
regulations of the country of origin.

10 9 8 7 6 5 4 3 2 1

To see our full range of titles visit **www.bloomsbury.com**

Acknowledgements
We would like to thank the staff and children of the following settings for their time
and patience in helping put this book together, including the use of a number of
photographs:

London Early Years Foundation, Emli Bendixen
Noah's Ark Pre-School
Edmondsley Primary School
Thomas More Roman Catholic Primary School
Woodhouse Community Primary School
The Arches Primary School
Cosy Foundation (Cosy Direct)

Also special thanks to Fee Bryce-Clegg & Kirstine Beeley

Contents

Introduction

One of the key life skills we need to empower our children in Early Years with is the skill of independence, both in their actions and their thinking.

To become independent, children have to be confident in their own abilities, otherwise they will remain over reliant on the support of other adults or their more confident peers.

Children's confidence grows through opportunities to try new things in a safe and supportive environment with lots of positive reinforcement for their success and strategies in place to support any failures they may have along the way.

Young children are on the whole very resourceful and very resilient and when left to their own devices or given opportunities to be independent they can often surprise us!

As practitioners we need to ensure that we are not only creating an environment and planning activities that are teaching children fundamental skills, we also need to give children opportunities to put those skills into practice on their own. This can be something as simple as filling a paint pot, to more complex activities like making bread. But all of these things (and more) are possible if children are given the correct input in the right environment and then given the chance to have a go.

In this book I have included some practical activities that you can try as well as some ideas for how you can organise your provision to support independent learning across all areas. Many of the activities in this book are already in use in a variety of settings up and down the country and are successfully inspiring even our youngest children to find their own sense of independence (with a little help from an adult or two!)

All of the activities were either created for, or inspired by, practice in a range of settings and have been tried and tested on real children!

Food allergy alert

When using food stuffs to enhance your outdoor play opportunties always be mindful of potential food allergies. We have used this symbol on the relevant pages.

Skin allergy alert

Some detergents and soaps can cause skin reactions. Always be aware of potential skin allergies when letting children mix anything with their hands and always provide lots of facilities to wash materials off after they have been in contact with the skin. Watch out for this symbol on the relevant pages.

Camping washing line

What you need:

- **Lengths of camping washing line**
- **Secure surfaces** (to attach the line to)

What to do:

1. Stretch out the camping washing line between two surfaces.

2. Attach your camping washing line to your walls securely following the manufacturer's instructions.

3. As the line is made from strong twisted elastic, there is no need for pegs or clips. Children can push fabric through the twists and it stays securely in place.

Taking it forward

- Put lengths of camping washing line at different heights.

- Use the washing lines outdoors between walls or trees.

What's in it for the children?

Children can use the washing line to make quick and simple dens and enclosures to promote the development of their imaginations and personalised play. Voiles work particularly well as they are lightweight as easy for children to manipulate.

Wall mounted paper rolls

What you need:

- Curtain pole
- Drill
- Screws
- Roll of paper waste or lining paper
- Mark making implements

What to do:

1. Cut the curtain pole down to the size required (approximately 1 metre long, or match the width of your paper rolls).

2. Mount the curtain pole on the wall at child height.

3. Thread the paper onto the pole.

4. Let the children access this mark making provision as they require it.

Taking it forward

- Set up several paper rolls around your setting.

- Use this approach outside as well as inside.

What's in it for the children?

Children who are at the gross motor stage of their mark making development need lots of big spaces in which to mark make. This idea supports that development as well as giving more dexterous children the opportunity to create large and small pieces of mark making.

Self service paint area

Powder paint

What you need:

- Powder paint
- Sugar shakers
- Small pots
- Paintbrushes
- Water in a pump dispenser

What to do:

1. Fill the sugar shakers with different colours of powder paint.

2. Show the children how to shake the dry powder into their pot.

3. Add water by squirting it from the dispenser.

4. Mix the paints up ready for use.

5. Let the children use the paint independently as required.

Taking it forward

- For a greater challenge try just giving the children primary colours and black and white paint and let them experiment to find all of the other colours that they might want to use.

What's in it for the children?

This gives the children a high level of independence and allows them to really experiment with the creative process of paint mixing. This sort of area works really well with children aged two years and upwards.

Ready mixed paint

What you need:

- **Pump dispensers** (like liquid soap)
- **Small pots**
- **Ready mixed paint**
- **Brushes and sponges**

What to do:

1. Decant the ready mixed paint into the pump dispensers.

2. Show the children how to squirt the paint into the pots or mixing palettes.

3. Let them use the paint independently for creative designs.

Taking it forward

- Talk to the children about how many pumps they should use at one time.

- Offer the children a range of other ingredients like flour or porridge oats that they can use to add thickness or texture to their paint.

What's in it for the children?

The children are not only learning about paint, texture and colour but this provision also supports them in being very self-sufficient.

Using real household objects

What you need:

- **Real household objects like knives, plates, glasses**

What to do:

1. Talk to the children about how household objects can be useful but also dangerous if not used properly.
2. Show the children how to use them safely.
3. Let the children have a go.

Taking it forward

- Explore a variety of household items.

What's in it for the children?

Sometimes children can perceive items they are not allowed to touch as exciting and this heightens their interest in them which can lead to inappropriate use. Explaining why certain items can be dangerous and then showing children will help to deter them from having a go by themselves.

✚ Health & Safety

Always make sure that an adult is present and that appropriate risk assessments have been carried out.

50 fantastic ideas for promoting independence

Using the washing machine

What you need:

- A washing machine
- Clothes and/or fabric
- Washing powder

What to do:

1. Let the children sort out the clothes and/or the fabric that they are going to wash.

2. Show them how to separate white and pale colours from dark colours and then put a suitable load into the machine.

3. Add the washing powder.

4. Set the appropriate programme, talking about the different temperature options and what they mean.

5. Start the machine.

Taking it forward

- Use the washing machine for other things such as dying fabric.

What's in it for the children?

Although it might not be something that they have had the opportunity to do before, most children will be very familiar with the use of the washing machine. Alongside a high level of independence, they will also have the opportunity to measure, act out familiar tasks, role-play and use and develop language.

Filling up the water tray

What you need:

- Sink
- Washing-up bowl or bucket
- Waterproof marker
- Water tray
- Liquid soap, food colouring, glitter
- Mop and bucket on stand by!

What to do:

1. Mark on the bowl or bucket the level that you would like the children to fill it to (make sure it is not too heavy or it will spill).

2. Show the children how to turn on the tap and fill to the mark.

3. Allow them to make as many trips as necessary to fill the water tray.

4. Add any extras like bubbles or glitter as required.

Taking it forward

- Try different ways to fill your water tray like running a hose pipe from the sink to the tray.

- Put the children on a rota for filling the water tray and making it part of their daily routine.

What's in it for the children?

You usually get lots of children who are eager to have a go at this. Not only are they taking responsibility for their environment they are also learning about capacity, weight and the movement of water.

3D labelling

What you need:

- Luggage labels or cards
- Storage boxes
- Resources small enough to fit on labels
- Super glue
- String

What to do:

1. Use one label or piece of card per resource to be labelled.

2. Take a piece of the resource or a picture of it and stick it to the label. You can stick small world resources such as farm animals as well as pieces of construction to your labels.

3. Attach the label to the box using the string.

Taking it forward

- Write in clear print on the back of the label to support the recognition of print and reading development.

What's in it for the children?

If the children are clear about what is inside the tubs and boxes in your space, they will spend less time sorting through them looking for what they want and more time using them to support their learning.

Health & Safety

This is an activity for adults to do, to label the resources clearly allowing children to access them independently. This increases their levels of independence, but super glue is for adults only!

Wide selection of resources

What you need:

- A range and variety of resources in each area of learning
- Storage that makes the resources easy to see and access

Taking it forward

- Make sure that there is always a range of resources available to support learning.

What's in it for the children?

The children are far more likely to engage in independent learning if there are a range of resources available that interest them. Learning the importance of getting something out and then putting it away again when you have finished is a key independence skill.

What to do:

1. Build up the selection of resources that you offer the children over time.

2. Store them in a way that is permanently accessible to the children. Display resources in low level containers such as baskets so that children can clearly see what is available and don't have to spend time 'sorting' before they can start.

3. Show the children how to use and replace the resources.

Dressing for outdoor play

What you need:

- Waterproofs
- Wellington boots
- Pegs
- Accessible storage

What to do:

1. Show the children how to put on their waterproofs by themselves by lying down and sliding into them.

2. Keep pairs of Wellington boots together by using a named peg for each pair.

3. Have an agreed routine for what the children do with the outdoor clothing when they come in (especially if they are wet and dirty).

Taking it forward

- Practise putting on and taking off outdoor clothing as part of an indoor activity until the children get the hang of it.

What's in it for the children?

The children will be more inclined to go out and play if they know how to get their outdoor clothing on and off easily. It also means that adults can use their time to support children's learning rather than dressing and undressing them.

Using video to record learning

What you need:

- Hand-held video device
- Laptop or computer for play back and storage

Taking it forward

- Use other simple video packages to add effects like music and animation to the videos the children have made.

What's in it for the children?

There is usually a high level of interest and enthusiasm when it comes to using a video recording device. The children have the opportunity to use ICT to share their thoughts, creativity and learning. Because the devices are small and simple to operate, they can do it without the support of an adult.

What to do:

1. Show the children how to operate the video device.
2. Talk about use of the device and the type of things it would be good to film.
3. Model the capturing of effective video and show the children what you have recorded.
4. Encourage the children to record themselves at work and play.
5. Let them play back and share what they have done with their peers.

Writing walls (indoors)

What you need:

- Clear wall space or display board at child height
- Lining paper (or similar)
- Means of attaching the paper to the board/wall
- Mark making implements

What to do:

1. Attach the plain paper to the wall or board to make a large mark-making space.

2. Encourage the children to use the mark-making materials to make marks or write.

3. Take photographs of the children mark making and then use the photographs and their marks to create a display.

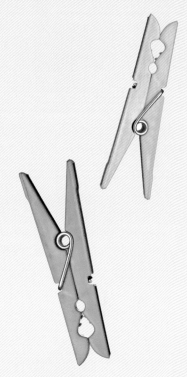

Taking it forward

- Put one of these mark-making walls or spaces in a number of areas of your setting. Not only are they great for your mark-making area, they also work really well in role-play and small world play.

What's in it for the children?

This sort of mark-making space not only supports children at each stage of their mark-making development, it also promotes the use of imagination and a shared experience.

Waterfall guttering

What you need:

- Access to an outdoor tap
- Hose pipe
- Plastic guttering
- Electric drill
- Screws

What to do:

1. Attach the guttering to the wall at child height.

2. Tilt the pieces of guttering at an angle so that the water can flow from one into the other.

3. Let the children use the hose to create a waterfall effect.

Taking it forward

- Add other resources that will roll or slide down the guttering such as toy cars, balls, ice cubes.

- Provide lots of different sized containers to catch the water at the bottom of the waterfall.

What's in it for the children?

The children are self managing the use of water outdoors and this control gives them a high level of independence. They will have the opportunity to learn about how water moves and can be controlled as well as having great fun!

Den making

What you need:

- Cardboard boxes
- Pegs
- Fabric
- String
- Tarpaulin
- Carpet inner tube
- Camping washing line

What to do:

1. Show the children how to construct a simple den using the resources.

2. Show them how to start by laying the floor.

3. Next they can find suitable resources to create the walls.

4. Finally they need to drape and dress the structure with fabric.

Taking it forward

- Make rainy day dens out of tarpaulins and builder's plastic.
- Use your den for having a snack, sharing a book or role-play.

What's in it for the children?

There are lots of key skills involved in den making. Once the children have got the hang of how to make a simple den they will be able to do it without the support of an adult. No two dens ever look the same and as different children play in them, the den changes shape and purpose depending on who is in it.

Outside painting station

What you need:

- Easels
- Paintbrushes
- Sponges and rollers
- Ready mixed paint in pump dispensers
- Powder paint in sugar shakers
- Water in a pump dispenser
- Variety of paper
- Washing-up bowl with water and soap
- Painting aprons (optional)

What to do:

1. Display your painting resources outside so that they are easily accessible for the children.

2. Set up a space with your washing-up bowl and water where the children can wash their resources once they have finished.

3. Encourage the children to use the outside painting station as an extension of the painting area indoors.

Taking it forward

■ Enhance this area with natural materials that could be added to the children's paintings or used to create transient art or sculpture.

What's in it for the children?

It is important that children have the opportunity to experience art outside and be able to record the things they do and see. If children are able to access this area unaided, it not only has a huge impact on their level of independence but also means that these areas do not have to be 'manned', freeing up staff to work with other children.

Places to be (outdoors)

What you need:

- Bushes
- Log piles
- Long grass
- Wild areas
- Tents
- Dens

What to do:

1. Leave grass to grow tall and wild in an area of your outdoor provision.
2. Allow bushes and trees to become bushy and overhang.
3. Create (or find natural) hillocks and dips.
4. Have a range of simple den making material/boxes available.
5. Let the children explore making their own outdoor dens.

Taking it forward

- Get the children to create more complex dens or hiding spaces that are made over time and become part of your long term outdoor provision.

What's in it for the children?

Children love to explore their outdoor environment. They often really like places where they can gather as small groups or hide. If you cannot create these 'places to be' using your natural landscape then it is worth having a go with den making equipment or even a willow structure.

Places to be (indoors)

What you need:

- Table
- MDF or plywood
- Saw
- Screws
- Screwdriver
- Cushions, rugs and blankets
- Rope ladder (optional)

What to do:

1. Use the table to create a space above and a space below.
2. Cut the MDF or plywood sheeting to make the sides, front, back and roof of your structure e.g. house.
3. Attach with screws and screwdriver.
4. 'Dress' the structure above and below the table to make a small cosy place to be.

Taking it forward

- Create other types of structure that are less rigid by using broom handles and fabric to make a tent effect.

What's in it for the children?

Children love to have small spaces to have quiet time, private or secretive. You can tap into their interest in this type of space and link it to lots of other areas of the curriculum e.g. these spaces can give a fantastic springboard to developing children's imagination, role play, small world, mark-making and mathematics to name but a few!

Self service snack

What you need:

- Toaster
- Tongs
- Plates, bowls and cups
- Cutlery
- Jugs
- Washing-up bowl
- Drying rack
- Tea towel

What to do:

1. Set up your snack area like a small kitchen or restaurant.

2. Put the toaster in a safe place and ensure the children do not touch the electric socket or toaster unattended.

3. Show the children how to toast bread safely.

4. Model how to spread butter, serve cereal and pour milk.

5. Agree a routine for what you do with any waste food at the end of snack time.

6. Demonstrate how to wash up, dry and put away.

- Theme your snack area like a café or restaurant and having waiters and waitresses to serve your 'customers'.

What's in it for the children?

The children are not only able to refuel at the snack area they are also learning key life skills about self sufficiency and personal and social interactions.

✚ Health & Safety

Ensure the electric socket is kept dry and away from the children's reach.

Real tools

What you need:

- **Selection of real tools**
  (you can buy fully working
  miniature versions)
- **Work bench**
- **Pieces of wood**

What to do:

1. Model to the children how the tools work and
   should be used.

2. Work alongside the children to show them how to
   use the tools safely.

3. Give the children lots of opportunity to use the
   tools independently but with supervision.

4. Allow the children to use the tools independently.
   For more ideas try *The Little Book of Woodwork*
   (Featherstone).

Taking it forward

- Have a range of tools available
  for use by the children both
  indoors and out.

What's in it for the children?

There is usually a high level of
engagement in this sort of activity
and children from a very young age
can be shown how to use tools
proficiently. As well as the high level
of independence, the children are
also re-enforcing lots of key skills
such as hand/eye co-ordination and
fine motor control.

 Health & Safety

Ensure the children's safety when
operating any tools.

Clearing up your own mess!

What you need:

- Dustpan
- Brushes
- Cloths
- Hoover

What to do:

1. Talk to the children about what you expect them to do if they make a mess.

2. Model to the children how you clean up following a spillage.

3. When the next spill happens work with the children and praise effort and successful outcomes.

4. Allow the children to have a try at cleaning up their mess on their own.

Taking it forward

- Set up cleaning stations around areas that are most likely to be messy like sand, water, paint and creative areas.

What's in it for the children?

The children are unlikely to clean up as well as you so you may need to do a quick whizz round once they have finished. However, letting children take responsibility for cleaning up their own mess gives them an introduction to key life skills as well as a high level of independence.

Collecting tubes

What you need:

- **Long tube with a lid** (often used for packaging crisps)
- **Wrapping paper or comics**
- **Sticky tape**
- **String or wool**
- **Luggage labels** (if personalising)

What to do:

1. Cover the tube in wrapping paper or pages of a comic.
2. Attach a piece of string to the top and bottom of the tube to create a shoulder strap.
3. Add a luggage label with the name and/or photograph of the child.
4. Fill the tube with resources or a challenge. You can put any sort of challenge into your tube. It could be a numeracy activity to complete, a mark-making resource to try out or a workshop resource to encourage children to make something by cutting, sticking and creating.
5. Allow the children to collect things of interest in their tube.

Taking it forward

- Have a number of tubes in lots of areas around your environment. Theme them to the interest of your children. Let the children take their tube and use it anywhere within your space that takes their fancy.

What's in it for the children?

Even though you might be in control of what goes into the tube the children get the feeling that they are very much in charge of when and where they complete the contents of their challenge tube. This is great for engagement as well as independence.

Milk crate table and chairs

What to do:

1. Show the children how to stack the milk crates to make a table and chairs.

2. Make your milk crate tables in a variety of sizes for one, two or ten children.

3. Use your milk crate tables indoors and out.

Taking it forward

- If you are going to use your milk crates for a table to draw or mark make on, make sure you have some clipboards for the children to rest on.

- Don't just stop at tables. Use the crates to make aeroplanes, towers or monsters. Whatever the children suggest!

What's in it for the children?

If children are able to create spaces to work whenever or wherever they want to, without having to ask an adult to do it for them, then they are far more likely to do it!

Message board

What you need:

- Coloured paper
- Laminating pouches and laminator
- Name cards
- Child height display space
- Sticky notes

What to do:

1. Cut the coloured paper into A6 rectangles, one for each child.
2. Add each child's name to one rectangle.
3. Laminate the rectangles.
4. Mount your rectangles together on your display space message board.
5. Encourage the children to send each other messages throughout the day by putting a sticky note on their friend's message board.
6. Adults can also use the board to send messages to children.

Taking it forward

- Add a photograph to the name on each board to help the non readers.
- You could enhance the display by adding talking postcards or talking tins so that children could leave a voice message.

What's in it for the children?

This is a great activity to promote communications as well as reading and mark making. Children who are non writers can leave a smiley face (or similar) for their friends.

Learning challenges

What you need:

- Paper
- Laminator and pouches
- Pictures/photographs of characters who reflect children's interests
- Talking tin/peg/postcard (optional)

What to do:

1. Write a challenge relating to a task that you would like the children to complete.
2. 'Dress' the challenge by basing it around a popular character from children's fiction.
3. Add pictures of the character to your challenge sheet.
4. Record the challenge onto a talking device to go alongside the paper version.

Taking it forward

- Have a series of smaller clues that eventually lead to the challenge card.
- Have a designated adult who children can ask for help with the challenge card if they get stuck.

What's in it for the children?

The children are more likely to engage independently with the challenge in the first place because it features a character in which they are interested. The use of a challenge card means that you can provide an extra layer of rigour to children's learning in continuous provision which they can access in the absence of an adult.

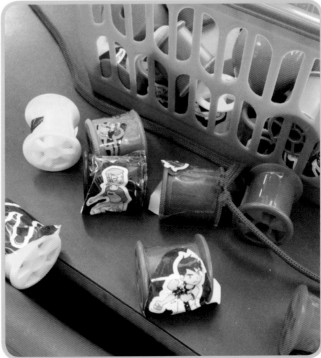

Funky fingers time

What you need:

- Carpet or table top space
- Piece of music that the children will relate to
- Resources to support the skill development

What to do:

1. Differentiate the resources so that children are given an activity that will help to promote independence.

2. Have all of the children working at the same time.

3. Put on your piece of music.

4. Get the children to carry out their activity in time with the music.

5. Get children kneading large pieces of dough to develop their upper arm and hands, threading pasta onto a string to develop hand/eye coordination and picking up lentils with tweezers to develop their pincer grip.

6. The activity ends when the music stops.

Taking it forward

- Have 'funky fingers' indoors for fine motor activities as well as outdoors for gross motor activities.

What's in it for the children?

We sometimes give children resources, such as scissors, that we want them to use in their independent work and exploration. The problem often occurs that the children's level of dexterity is not high enough to enable effective use of the resource. Funky fingers is an opportunity to practise and develop that dexterity and activity in a short, funky and fun way. Then children can be truly independent in their work.

Talking postcard instruction

What you need:

- Recordable postcard
- Dry wipe marker

What to do:

1. Record your activity idea, prompt or question onto a recordable postcard.
2. Write an instruction onto the front of the card that repeats or supports the talk you have recorded.
3. Leave the talking postcard in the environment for children to access and use independently.

Can you make a sandwich?

Taking it forward

- Get the children to record the tasks and activities onto the postcards as they are more likely to talk about them and complete what is asked of them if they have been instrumental in creating the card.

What's in it for the children?

Children have both visual and verbal support to help them to complete an activity or challenge. This increased level of independence means that the adults in the setting can focus on supporting learning in other ways.

Personalised labelling

What you need:

- **Camera**
- **Printer**
- **Laminator**
- **Paper** (for speech bubbles)
- **Marker pen**

What to do:

1. Decide which aspects of your environment and the provision would benefit from a label.
2. Take photographs of children from the setting giving a visual clue to what is going to be on the written label.
3. Write in a speech bubble an explanation of what is happening in the photo.
4. Laminate the photo and the speech bubble and put them in the appropriate part of your environment.

Taking it forward

- Not only use the children in the environmental labelling but also use images of the adults who work in the space.

What's in it for the children?

The children are more likely to engage with the labelling because it features their significant adults, themselves and their peers. The photographs will also help them to interpret what the print says, thereby increasing the potential for independent learning.

Self-esteem builder

What you need:

- **Photos of the children in your setting**
- **Name cards** (optional)
- **Peg** (optional)

What to do:

1. Laminate at least three photos of each child.
2. Add a name card to the bottom of the photo (optional).
3. Either attach the photo and name card to a clothes peg or use a peg to easily attach the photo to children's work or creations.
4. Ask the children to label their completed work (and display) by using their photos.

Taking it forward

- Add photo pegs to drying work, models, mark making etc as well as display.

What's in it for the children?

Not all children will recognise their own name, never mind anyone else's. What they do recognise however is their own image and the image of others. This system of identifying work and labelling displays allows children who cannot write their name to make it clear which work is theirs without having to wait for an adult to write for them. This is not only good for their independence; it is also great for their self-esteem.

Tinkering

What you need:

- Various everyday objects that children can safely take to bits and 'tinker' with to find out how they work and how they are made
- Appropriate tools

What to do:

1. Check any equipment that you give children to tinker with to ensure that there are no dangerous parts.

2. Explain to the children that what they are going to tinker with no longer works which is why they can take it apart.

3. Provide as many real tools as you can for them to use.

4. Monitor their tinkering to ensure that there is no risk from small parts.

Taking it forward

- Create a 'tinker table' where children have constant access to things that they can deconstruct.

What's in it for the children?

The children are learning lots about how things are made and also how to take them apart. Alongside firing their interest and imagination, tinkering is good for developing children's fine motor skills and hand/eye co-ordination.

Health & Safety

Ensure children's safety in using tools. Make sure any items they are investigating are safe for them to explore.

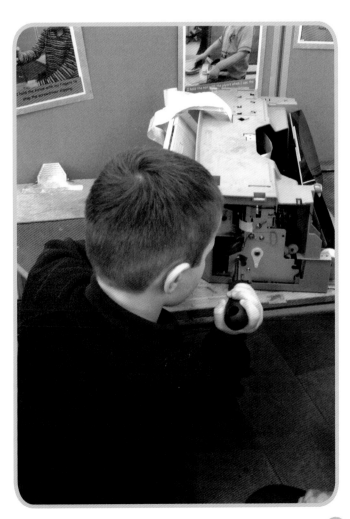

Make your own bread

What you need:

- Bread maker
- Ingredients
- Instructions on how to make bread in photographic form

How to Make Raisin Bread

What to do:

1. On the first few occasions work alongside the children as they follow the instructions.

2. Encourage the children to make the bread using the instructions while you watch but don't intervene unless it is necessary.

Taking it forward

- Apply this concept not only to other forms of cooking and baking but to other areas of your setting.

What's in it for the children?

The children are learning key life skills as well as showing a high level of independence. The key is that the children are following instructions but without adult intervention.

 Health & Safety

An adult will need to put the dough in and take it out of the bread maker.

Phonetic labelling

What you need:

- Lots of pieces of card in different sizes
- Mark-making implements

What to do:

1. Get the children to use their phonetic spelling to label key areas of your environment.

2. Use any errors that they make in their labelling as a teaching point for future phonic sessions.

Taking it forward

- Get the children to write instructions for how to use the provision or play a game.

What's in it for the children?

In the early stages of their reading and writing development, most children apply a very simple phonic strategy to reading and spelling. This means that the labels that they write are easier for their peers to read and act upon as they are phonetically spelled. This type of phonetic labelling allows children to access provision independently because they are able to understand the instruction.

Storage of outdoor resources

What you need:

- Polyurethane greenhouse
- Storage baskets or boxes
- Themed resources
- Heavy weights

What to do:

1. Assemble the polyurethane greenhouse as per the instructions.

2. Place the resources into the storage baskets or boxes.

3. Place the boxes on the shelves within the greenhouse.

4. Weigh down the bottom of the greenhouse with a weight or heavy object.

Taking it forward

- Have a number of these in different sizes dotted around your outdoor environment.

What's in it for the children?

These greenhouses are a relatively cheap way of being able to get resources outside and keep them dry and from being blown away! This in turn allows children to access a great deal more of the outdoor provision independently. If children have responsibility for managing their own resources and are given the support to help achieve that goal, then they will be able to make individual choices and foster high levels of independence.

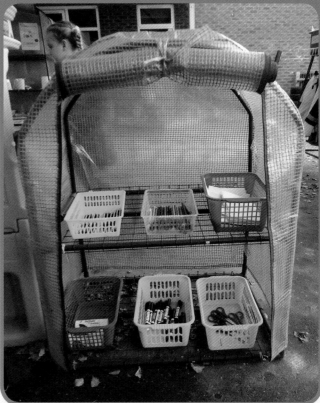

What you need:

- **Any small boxes, drawers or pouches** (one per child)
- **Photographs** (for each child)
- **Name cards** (for each child)

What to do:

1. Use the boxes, drawers or pouches to create an individual space for each child.

2. The children can keep things that are important or special to them in their special space.

Taking it forward

- Encourage the children to bring in photos from home of other key people in their life. This can help to support their emotional wellbeing in your setting.

What's in it for the children?

The more personal a space is to a child the higher their levels of emotional wellbeing are likely to be. This has a significant impact on their readiness to learn. Over time children will gain ownership of their space when it is filled with their work, activities and experiences, but a small space that is just for them can really help the personalisation.

Engagement/activity boxes

What you need:

- Cardboard boxes
- Wrapping paper themed to children's specific interests
- Resources that are linked to the children's stage of development

What to do:

1. 'Dress' the box by covering it in wrapping paper to match the children's interests.
2. Fill the box with appropriate resources.
3. Place the box within your setting for the children to access in continuous provision.

Taking it forward

- 'Dressing' other aspects of your provision around the interests of children to heighten the likelihood of them accessing specific resources outside of adult-led teaching time.

What's in it for the children?

In continuous provision, children tend to re-visit activities and experiences that they know they can do easily. A box that has been 'dressed' to match their interests is more likely to get their attention and if it has been filled with appropriate resources, will take their learning forward.

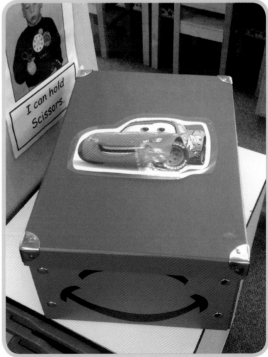

Deconstructed role-play

What you need:

- Large and small cardboard boxes
- Baskets
- Milk and bread crates
- Cardboard tubes
- Fabric
- Hats and mirrors

What to do:

1. Make a collection of open-ended resources like boxes and tubes.

2. Place them in a large open space.

3. Encourage the children to use their imagination to turn these open-ended resources into specific play experiences that are meaningful to them.

Taking it forward

■ Create a deconstructed role-play area indoors and out.

What's in it for the children?

If children do not have a great deal of personal experience of a role-play space that they have set up, then they are going to struggle to play in it without adult support, often reverting to playing 'house' or 'super heroes'. A deconstructed role-play area supports any play theme because of its open-ended potential.

What you need:

- Basket or box
- Resources that are themed around a specific interest e.g. builder, babies or vet
- Books to support and enhance the theme
- Mark making materials

What to do:

1. Identify themes that you wish to cover in your role-play.
2. Identify key areas of interest for children that they have expressed through their play.
3. Create an enhancement basket of resources to support these themes.
4. Take the enhancement baskets into your deconstructed role-play area to support children's learning.

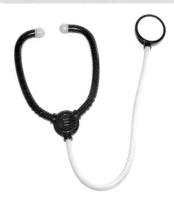

Taking it forward

- It is good to always have a 'home' enhancement box in your deconstructed role-play area as this is a familiar play experience for all children.

What's in it for the children?

Enhancement baskets support the development and consolidation of children's play in an area that they are familiar with or interested in. If an adult has created an enhancement basket to support a taught theme that the children are not as familiar with such as 'the vet's' then the adult can use these resources in the deconstructed role-play area to introduce appropriate language without over theming.

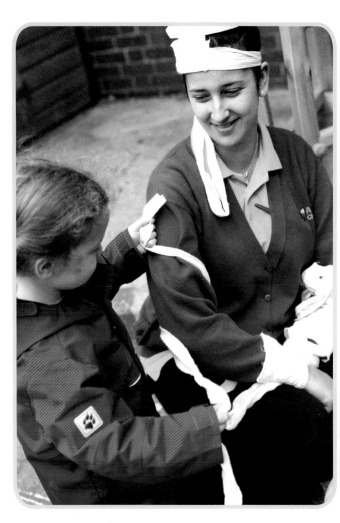

Personalised display

What you need:

- **Photos of your children relating to the subject of the display**
- **Laminator and pouches**
- **Talking postcard** (optional)

What to do:

1. Photograph your children demonstrating a setting rule, an action (like rolling dough) or as part of a learning display (like an alphabet or number line).
2. Laminate the photographs.
3. Display these at child eye height for maximum impact.
4. Add a talking postcard to further support the learning.

Taking it forward

- Putting personalised display in all areas of your setting.

What's in it for the children?

Children in early years tend to be very ego driven and find themselves more engaging than anything else! We can capitalise on this engagement by including them in our teaching display. This sort of display also really helps to personalise their space.

Investigation areas

What you need:

- Table top space
- Number of open-ended/ interesting resources that will inspire children
- Display themed around specific interests of the group of children that you particularly want to engage
- Prompt cards/talking tins

What to do:

1. Create an exciting space with some resources available for open-ended investigation.

2. Enhance your area with written challenges and question prompts written or record them on a talking tin or postcard.

?

?

Taking it forward

- Get the children to generate questions and record them for other children and adults to answer or discover.

What's in it for the children?

Ideally we want our children to be inspired and intrigued by the areas of learning that we create. If they are interested in a particular space they will spend a great deal of time in it and a significant amount of self-initiated independent learning can take place.

Open-ended interest activity

What you need:

- Children's ideas
- Open-ended resources
- Paper and pens to document the journey

What to do:

1. Through talk and discussion, identify children's passions and interests.
2. Use this interest to set up an activity that allows them to experiment and try out their ideas.
3. Document their progress.
4. Review the process at the end.

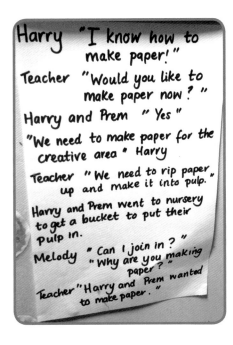

Harry "I know how to make paper!"

Teacher "Would you like to make paper now?"

Harry and Prem "Yes"

"We need to make paper for the creative area" Harry

Teacher "We need to rip paper up and make it into pulp."

Harry and Prem went to nursery to get a bucket to put their pulp in.

Melody "Can I join in?"
"Why are you making paper?"

Teacher "Harry and Prem wanted to make paper."

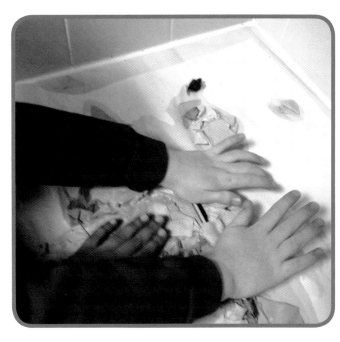

Taking it forward

- Create individual as well as group projects within your setting. Some might last for a relatively short length of time but some will go on and on…

What's in it for the children?

Children are often very inspired by their own ideas and interests and need to explore. If we can capitalise on this enthusiasm then we are far more likely to get higher level learning.

Challenge bags

What you need:

- Small gift or party bags themed around the interest of the children you are targeting
- Laminated labels for personalising the bags
- Differentiated contents that target specific activities or learning

What to do:

1. Identify children that you would like to target with a specific challenge.
2. Choose a theme for your challenge bag that will appeal to the child you want to challenge.
3. Put their challenge resources into the bag. The sort of challenges that you could put in could be linked to re-enforcing key skills that you have taught. It could be consolidation of a maths concept or an interesting object to investigate and explore.
4. Label the bag with their name and/or photograph.
5. Put/hide the bag within your provision and challenge the children concerned to find the bag and complete the task that is in it.

Taking it forward

- Use a challenge bag for individual children or groups.
- Use the challenge bags in your indoor and outdoor environment.

What's in it for the children?

You are helping the children to complete challenges within the provision rather than pulling them out of their play. Children also like the fact that they have a challenge that is individual to them and are therefore more motivated to complete it independently.

Activity back packs

What you need:

- Children's back packs themed around popular children's TV characters
- Activities and resources linked to assessment, learning and discovery

Taking it forward

- Creating more generic back packs like a counting pack or a drawing pack.
- Label the back packs with children's photographs to target a more specific need.

What's in it for the children?

The children usually love the idea of taking away a back pack to explore. They are more likely to complete or use what has been placed inside the back pack because they have engaged with it in the first place.

What to do:

1. Identify groups of children by their interests.
2. Theme the content of the back pack around the needs of the children who are interested in that character.
3. Tell the children that they can take a back pack whenever they want and explore the contents.
4. Children return the back pack to an adult once they have finished with it.

Time to explore

What you need:

- Extended periods of continuous provision in your day
- Open-ended resources that can be interpreted in a number of ways
- Open-ended provision both indoors and out

What to do:

1. Plan to have several periods of continuous provision in your day that allow children to investigate and explore.

2. Have a range of open-ended resources available for children to interpret depending on their experience.

3. Avoid pulling children out of provision to come and work with an adult, try taking the learning into play

Taking it forward

- Observing children in this sort of play will help you to determine what interests them, what they already know and what you need to plan to take their learning forward.

What's in it for the children?

The children will benefit from long periods of uninterrupted play where they can independently investigate and explore their environment. They can apply skills that they have already learned and test and practise theories about how the world works.

Small world storage

What you need:

- Low open trays or baskets
- Open shelving
- Photographic and text-rich labelling
- Specific and open-ended ambiguous resources
- Fabric and small den making equipment

What to do:

1. Categorise your small world play into individual components.

2. Put each set of components into a low open basket or tray for maximum visibility.

3. Label each basket with photographs and text.

4. Include small world resources that have been created as a specific object such as a house and also open-ended resources that could be anything such as a wooden block or a coconut shell.

Taking it forward

- Create a number of small world stations throughout your environment so that children can combine small world play into other areas of learning.

What's in it for the children?

You want children in small world play to spend the majority of their time developing their play and not sorting through boxes to find what they need before they can start.

Small world mats and shelters

What you need:

- A variety of large and small mats in different colours, shapes and textures
- A range of fabric in different weights colours and textures
- Small joining resources such as paper clips, pegs and string
- Natural construction materials such as sticks, twigs, wood slices

What to do:

1. Provide a range of mats as part of your small provision.

2. Place the fabric and shelter construction resources in easy to access containers.

3. Children can make their own real and fantasy play environments, using the resources to create fields, hills, rivers, volcanoes and fantasy worlds to name but a few! When children have the opportunity to use their higher order thinking skills and creativity to support their play they are less likely to rely on adult intervention and support.

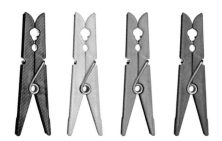

Taking it forward

- Enhance your outdoor small world provision even further by providing a range of textures such as sand, shingle, bark and grass for the children to play with small world equipment in. This can be done in small containers or tyres.

What's in it for the children?

Part of small world play is creating a version of a 'real' environment for small world characters to exist in. The provision of textured mats helps children to create 'real' play spaces. It also allows for individual and group work depending on the size of the mat.

Outdoor water play

What you need:

- Access to an outdoor tap or water butt with a tap
- Range of large scale resources like buckets, tubes, scoops, ladles etc.
- Waterproof clothing and Wellington boots

What to do:

1. Model to the children how to use the tap appropriately and safely.

2. Allow the children to self manage the flow of water from the tap.

3. Ensure that you provide a range of resources that offer different and complimentary skill development from the water play that you provide indoors.

4. Prepare to get wet!

Taking it forward

- Large scale water play is only really limited by space and children's imagination. If the children's play becomes repetitive then give them some water based challenges to solve.

What's in it for the children?

The children will enjoy the independence of being able to control the flow of the water. This often results in high-level engagement and the potential for high-level attainment. If the adult has got their resourcing right then the opportunities for independent learning are huge.

Simple sewing

What you need:

- **Binka or hessian**
- **Embroidery thread or wool**
- **Large eye needles** (metal or plastic)
- **Templates and designs**

What to do:

1. Show the children how to thread their needles.
2. Start with a simple running stitch (in and out).
3. Attempt a cross stitch with the more adventurous children.
4. Draw around or trace outlines of simple interesting shapes such as cartoon characters or dinosaurs and let the children stitch around their outlines.

Taking it forward

- For children who are not yet dexterous enough to co-ordinate a needle and thread you can use a single hole punch to punch around the outline of a picture or design and then show them how to thread through the holes with wool or string.

What's in it for the children?

This is the sort of activity that doesn't need to be completed in one go. It can be revisited on a number of occasions until it is complete. Once children have mastered the basics they can enjoy this activity without the support of an adult.

Outdoor investigation station

What you need:

- Fabric bags, pockets or pouches
- Magnifying glasses
- Collecting jars
- Mark making materials
- Clipboards
- Cups, bowls, spoons and containers
- Cushions and mats

What to do:

1. Set up your investigation area in an open space outside where the children can have clear access to all the resources.

2. Fill your bags and pouches with tools to help the children investigate and explore the outdoor space.

3. Encourage them to record their findings and experiments.

✚ Health & Safety

Ensure appropriate heath and safety assessment has been carried out in any area outside where children will be allowed to pick up and collect resources.

Taking it forward

■ For extra independence you could also add a self service snack/drink area to your investigation station. Use water containers with a tap and a table for the snacks.

What's in it for the children?

Children will have the opportunity to work on their own or in a group to investigate their outdoor surroundings. They will be able to collect, examine and create the things that they find.

Make your own...

What to do:

1. Model with the children the sequence of instructions for creating the item in question. (In the photograph the child is making her own play dough).

2. Allow the children to have a go under adult supervision.

3. When you think they know what they are doing, leave out as part of your continuous provision.

flour

spoon

Taking it forward

- Having multiple 'Make your own...' areas throughout your environment.

What's in it for the children?

Very young children are capable of high levels of independence, it is often just that they are not given enough opportunities to demonstrate that ability. When they are able to make things for themselves, they not only learn from the process of making but they also gain confidence and independence.

Silhouettes with a difference

What you need:

- Camera
- Coloured printer
- Laminator and pouches
- Scissors
- Adhesive backed plastic

What to do:

1. Take aerial view photographs of the contents of pots, tins and boxes you have in your provision.

2. Enlarge your photograph so it matches the 'real' size of the base of the container you have taken a photograph of.

3. Stick the photograph to the shelf or surface where the resource is stored.

4. Cover the photograph with sticky backed plastic.

Taking it forward

- Use these silhouettes in all areas of your provision both indoors and out.

What's in it for the children?

Traditionally silhouettes have been black outlines of the base of storage containers (hence the name) to help children to put resources away correctly. As a lot of resources in early years are stored in containers that are round, square or rectangular this can result in the wrong resource being returned to the wrong place. This form of labelling means that the children can be far more effective at managing their space independently. Providing you can get them to tidy up, that is!

Display your own work

What you need:

- **Display board at child height**
- **Backing paper** – themed or neutral depending on the area
- **Netting**
- **Staple gun**
- **Pegs of various sizes or pegs with photographs of the children**

Top tip ★

Get the children to use photo pegs to help to identify who has produced the masterpieces on display!

What to do:

1. Back the board with your chosen backing paper.

2. Cover the backing paper loosely with net.

3. Secure the net to the board around the outside and in the middle.

4. Encourage the children to peg their work to the board when they have finished it.

Taking it forward

- You can extend this idea by hanging large pieces of net from the ceiling and getting the children to peg their finished work onto that.

- Outdoors, apply the same idea to garden trellis which can be used to help you to divide your outdoor space as well as create an area for display.

What's in it for the children?

Rather than putting their work into a tray or back in their drawer the children have the opportunity to display their work. If they use a photo peg then everyone will know who the work belongs to.